I0518580

" Elohims"

(Release date: September 11th 2025)

ISBN: 979-8-9992734-1-3

Author: Lindbergh Sedacy Sr

Elohims

By Lindbergh Sedacy Sr

INTRODUCTION

About the Author: Lindbergh Sedacy

Lindbergh Sedacy is a spiritual teacher, author, and guide who has dedicated his life to sharing advanced insights and enlightenment principles with others. Through his writings and teachings, he offers a unique perspective on the nature of reality, the human condition, and the path to spiritual awakening.

With a deep understanding of the mysteries of existence, Lindbergh Sedacy's work is characterized by its clarity, wisdom, and compassion. He writes upon a wide range of spiritual awakening results synthesizing them into a coherent and practical framework for personal growth and transformation.

Through "Elohim," Lindbergh Sedacy invites readers to join him on a journey of self-discovery and spiritual exploration. His book offers practical guidance, profound insights, and inspiring stories, all designed to help readers awaken to their true nature and live a more authentic, meaningful, and fulfilling life.

As a spiritual guide, LindberghSedacy's work is not about dogma or doctrine, but about empowering individuals to tap into their own inner wisdom and potential. His teachings encourage readers to question, seek, and explore, trusting in their own inner guidance and intuition.

DISCLAIMER

purpose is to explore spiritual vision, growth, and awakening through a fictional lens.

DEDICATION

Spirituality is all of us are one; I am another you and you are another me and what bines us together as one is love and in love separation is an illusion let us reflect on each other as interconnectedness in the Flower of Life especially one mindset one faith one movement one belief that individually we are Elohim Gods but in togetherness we are One body One God in every aspect over the earth galaxy and universe.

Lindbergh Sedacy teaches us that we are all interconnected, and I reflect you and you reflect me. Love is the binding force that unites us, rendering separation an illusion that scattered us rendering us disorganized powerless and weak.

Let's recognize our interconnectedness, reflected in the sacred geometry of the Flower of Life. Together, we can embody a unified mindset, of shared faith, and we can collectively join a movement, rooted in the understanding that individually, we are sparks of the divine, but together, we are one body, one consciousness, embracing the entirety of the earth, galaxy, and universe.

I believe King Solomon wives were all from beyond the ice walls; his wives taught him everything he knew because they arrived from higher levels of civilizations. King Solomon's knowledge was so advanced above the average people that they all believe he was out of his mind because they didn't have a clue; couldn't understand most things he was talking about and so he was branded to be crazy. When actor Mr. Terrence Howard first began explaining the flower of life every one didn't have a clue of what he was explaining and taught that he was out of his mind "crazy"; the same attitude when most begin reading my spiritual awakening books most couldn't relate and branded me out of my mind I am accused of being crazy. Teaching a higher realm is next to impossible for an average person to relate with its understanding.

(1 Corinthians 2:12-15).

Author Lindbergh Sedacy narrated that King Solomon's wives were from advanced civilizations beyond this known world, and they imparted their knowledge to him. As a result, King Solomon understood far surpassed that of the average and learned person, leading many to believe he was out of touch with reality. They couldn't grasp the depth of his insights, and he was often misunderstood. Similarly, when actor Mr. Terrence Howard began explaining the Flower of Life. Many were perplexed and thought he was eccentric. I've experienced a similar reaction to my spiritual awakening books; most people struggle to relate and often label me as unconventional. Teaching about higher realms can be challenging, as it's difficult for those without similar experiences to understand (1 Corinthians 2:12-15).

Please be kind to one another:

For those who've walked hand in hand for decades, only to find themselves apart in the twilight of life, I urge you to reconsider. It's never too late to forgive. Let go of past hurts and reunite with the one who shares your heart. The flame of love may have dimmed, but the embers remain, waiting to be fanned into a warm, golden glow. Love isn't just a feeling; it's a cosmic force that resonates deep within our souls, a frequency of positive energy that transcends time and space. Why can't we see that love is the very essence of our existence, a divine spark that ignites our hearts and minds? It's not about the physical expression of love; it's about unconditional acceptance, the unwavering commitment, and the profound connection that binds two souls together. True love isn't meant to fade; it's meant to endure, withstand the tests of time, and flourish until our final breath. Let's give love a chance to overflow with goodness, heal the wounds of the past, and bring us closer together. May

4

the blessings of Yahweh be upon you, guiding you to hold dear the one who holds your heart... Amien.

BRINGING IT FOREWORD

Elohim are independent individuals who will stop at nothing to reach to the peoples with the ultimate truths of Yahweh's guidance and salvation. They will sacrifice themselves to deliver the messages of truths to the general public. John 3:16.

The Elohim are unwavering messengers who tirelessly share the ultimate truths of Yahweh's guidance and salvation with humanity. With unrelenting dedication, they sacrifice themselves to deliver these life-changing messages to the public, as reflected in John 3:16: 'For God so loved the world that he gave his begotten Sons and daughters, that whoever believes in Yahweh shall not perish but have eternal life.

People are into their own private reasons why they do stuff.

Why be a street preacher? Why go to church? Mostly does they believe that they will be blest with prosperity for doing so.

I write books because of my passion joy love in sharing these vital spiritually awakening messages and because the universe compels me my work will save lives and help many to understand the difference between religion feeding the wine press which is the deception of the business of church around recruiting membership based on selling salvation, vs spirituality the waken Christ consciousness recognizes to be the return of Christ in individuals living all over the earth; now Christ can be everywhere in every place at the same time.

Around a hundred and forty four thousands peoples out of nine billion peoples from the earth shall be selected in the harvest called the rapture; these selected saints will disappear never to be seen again, they'll be taken to a safe haven underground away from the surface of the earth, just before the destruction comes upon the earth, taken where they'll be sheltered feed protected nourishes from the atomic missiles destruction above while they'll bunkered down underground until the calamities above be over passed. Won't emerge until after centuries have passed and the radiation levels on the surface of earth subsided; then out from the underground, out of the ashes, out of the fires we shall rise to an empty uninhibited earth to a new reset a new dawn a new heaven and earth within dwells righteousness Isaiah 65: 17-25.

People have their own personal reasons for their actions. Some become street preachers or attend church, often believing that these actions will bring them prosperity and blessings. I write books because of my passion for sharing spiritually awakening messages that can save lives and help people understand the distinction between religion and spirituality. The awakened Christ consciousness, which recognizes the return of Christ within individuals worldwide, is a profound concept that transcends traditional religious boundaries. According to biblical prophecy, a select group of 144,000 individuals will be chosen from a global population of billions and taken to a safe haven underground before the impending destruction. There, they will be sheltered, nourished, and protected from the catastrophic events unfolding above. After centuries pass and the radiation levels subside, they will emerge into a new era, symbolizing a new heaven and a new earth, where righteousness dwells (Isaiah 65:17-25).

PREFACE

In the beginning, there existed a world unlike any other. A world where giants roamed the earth, and ancient civilizations thrived. The Nephilim, beings of great power and knowledge, arrived on the scene, bringing with them advanced technology and a thirst for domination. They cut down the giant trees, suffocating the giants, and a great flood reshaped the earth's surface.

From the ashes of this cataclysmic event, a new world emerged. The indigenous peoples, the Children of Eden, survived and thrived in this new environment. But the Nephilim's experiments with animals, birds, fish, and insects would change the course of history forever.

As we embark on this journey, we will explore the mysteries of the past, the secrets of the Elohim, and the truth about the world's true history. Join me as we uncover the hidden narratives and reveal the untold stories of our ancient ancestors.

The second coming of Christ symbolizes a transformation of a higher spiritual ascended consciousness; that's totally different from the destruction of all wicked people set for 11/09/2112. The coming of Christ and the destruction of the world are two different events.

No man knows the day and hour of the rapture, but the destruction of the wicked governments and people has a mandate on November 9th 2112.

Why is it that so many people cannot see themselves as gods, so I asked you to explain: 1 John 3:1-3.

1 John 3:1-3 describes the relationship between humanity and God, highlighting the love and identity that come with being a child of God. Here's a breakdown:

1. Children of God: The passage emphasizes that believers are called "children of God" due to being made created in his own image and

likeness. This identity comes from God referring to his son as God who created the worlds Hebrews 1:1,8.

2. Unknown to the world: The world doesn't recognize themselves to be children of God because people don't know themselves within to be transporting God Himself. This highlights the spiritual divide between those who know God and those who don't know that we are joining God. 1 Corinthians 6:16-19.

3. Future revelation: The passage mentions that what humans hasn't been able to understand yet, that at Chust second coming we will be we will become like him represents Christ appearance, they will be like Him. This points to the transformative power of Christ's return.

4. Purification: Those who have become ascended ascension of Christ purify themselves, reflecting Elohim Gods. This emphasizes the importance of seeing yourself as chist have that he and God are one, motivated ourselves in the hope of being like Christ.

Overall, these verses encourage us to live out our identity as children of God seeing ourselves for who and what we really are gods, embracing our divinity that comes through the knowledge of self we are more than children of God we are gods (JOHN 3:2; Isaiah 56:5).

The truth is to smash, eat, and drink be merry today in the moment because tomorrow isn't promised. One by one, we have been taken away, by premature deaths, and gone too soon. So many living dead peoples who stand exposed in nakedness of not elevating their frequency to their Higher Most High Selves and are targeted by the grim reaper who suddenly arrives and snach away your breathe, pray I say pray without ceasing for the light the star of truths to arise in your heart too bring about your ascension and be prepared to be picked up by the time machine of Eden and be restored to the glory that you once were long before the underworld became a place of sorrows and darkness .yes, back to Eden, we'll be given back everything that we've lost and was taken from us in this underworld; please comfort one another with helping hopeful encouraging words.

The truth is, we should cherish every day as if it's our last. Eat, drink, and be merry in the present moment because tomorrow isn't promised. One by one, we're being taken away, often by premature deaths, leaving us with the painful reality of those who are gone too soon.

Many people are walking around, yet they're spiritually dead, unaware of their true potential and not elevating their frequency to connect with their Higher Selves. They're vulnerable to the forces that can suddenly take their breath away.

I urge you to pray without ceasing for the light of truth to arise in your heart. As you ascend to your inner universe, you'll be prepared to return to the glory that once was yours long before the underworld became a place of sorrow and darkness.

Yes, we'll return to Eden, and everything that was lost and taken from us will be restored. In the meantime, let's comfort one another with hopeful, encouraging words. Let's help each other rise above the challenges of this world and reconnect with our true selves.

TABLE OF CONTENT MESSAGE

Bible Verses using EL= Elohim....let's in place of the elders and brothers we'll use the word: Elohim.

Acts 14:2-5

But the white Jews who refused to believe stirred up the Gentiles and poisoned their minds against the elohim brothers. So they spent considerable time there, speaking boldly for Yahweh, who confirmed the message of his grace by enabling them to do miraculous signs and wonders. The people of the city were divided; some sided with the white Jews, others with the black Elohim apostles. There was a plot afoot among both the heathens Gentiles and the white Jewish people, together with their leaders, to mistreat the black Elohims and stone them.

Titus 1:5.

The reason I left you in Crete was that you might put in order what was left unfinished and appoint Elohim in every town, as I directed you.

James (JASPER) 5:14.

Is anyone among you sick? Let them call the Elohim of the church to pray over them and anoint them with oil in the name of Yahweh.

1 Peter 5:5.

In the same way, you who are younger, submit yourselves to your elohim elders. All of you, clothe yourselves with humility toward one another because, "God opposes the proud but shows favor to the humble."

Revelation 4:4.

Around the throne were twenty-four Elohim elders, and seated on the thrones were twenty-four Elohim elders, dressed in white robes with golden crowns on their heads.

In place of "elders," I've use "Elohim" in some of these verses of context:

In Acts 14:2-5, we could discuss the role of Elohim in spreading the message of God's grace.

In Titus 1:5, instead of "elders," we might consider "appointing Elohim representatives in every town.""

In James 5:14, "Let them call the Elohim of the church to pray over them."

- In 1 Peter 5:5, "Submit yourselves to the Elohim, clothe yourselves with humility."

Revelations 4:4 describes the twenty-four Elohim seated around the throne.

Our minds are the reflection of the external universe, and our bodies are the reflection of our external earth; We are the creators of every external deities including the Anunnaki and the heavens and the earth. We are the Gods as within, so is it reflected outwardly from us? Without us, there isn't anything made that is made. If the devils reign and kill us all, everything externally will collapse because everything externally is a manifestation of our inner light, our inner thoughts and intentions. Everything externally is a hologram of our collective inner selves. We are the only thing real nothing exists outside of ourselves we keep it all together; By not compromising we do not worship any external deities we do not called any external deities God we do not bow worship nor called any external deities lord. We do not take or make any images of anything external and worship it, for collectively, we are one God.

Our minds reflect the external universe, and our bodies reflect the earth. As creators, we manifest external realities, including deities like the Anunnaki and the very fabric of the heavens and earth. The principle "as within, so without" suggests that our inner world is mirrored outwardly. If chaos and destruction reign externally, it's a reflection of our collective inner state when the earth floods it's our personal tears being reflected external. Everything external is a hologram of our inner light, thoughts, and intentions. Ultimately, we are the only reality; nothing exists outside of ourselves. We are the cohesive force that holds everything together. By recognizing our collective divinity, we don't worship external deities or idols. Instead, we acknowledge our oneness as the singular, all-encompassing God. We don't create images to worship, for we are the embodiment of the divine, collectively and individually.

This is what spirituality is all about. It focuses on you, the Elohim brothers and sisters, and spirituality, which also begins with you and ends with you. When you do not see yourself as a god then you are an average human being who arrived out of the water as a program sim but when you acknowledge yourself to be an Elohim God walking in the flesh on earth then you are an Awaken Christ consciousness you are the embodiment of the second coming of Christ; please gather yourselves for the rapture to be taken up yes beam me upward for Eden is my home and Eden is coming to take me away to safety because I am an Elohim God and shall be protected by any means nessiary, you are the apple of Yahweh's eyes and shall be preserved at any and all cost. Elohim means Gods, Psalms 82:6.

Let's break down the concept of Elohim brothers and sisters being referred to as "gods" in John 10:34:

1. Elohim: In Hebrew, "Elohim" is a term used to describe One God , but it can also refer to humans who represent Gods divinity and authority.

2. Psalm 82:6: This verse says, "I said, 'You are gods; you are all sons of the Most High.'" Here, humans are referred to as "gods" or "elohim" because they have a connection to God's authority.

3. John 10:34: Jesus quotes Psalm 82:6, saying, "Is it not written in your Law, 'I said, you are gods?'" The Bible uses this scripture to defend Christ claim of being the Son of God, arguing that if humans can be called "gods" due to their connection with God who reign with them, humans transport God within, and by looking at him in his Most High Self then you're witnessing God in the flesh and for saying I and my father are one, he shouldn't be considered a blasphemer. The religious authority wanted to stone Christ to die for linking himself to be one with God.

4. Implications: This passage highlights the potential connection between humans and the divine. It suggests that humans can have a divine nature and represent God, Hebrews 13:2.

In the context of Elohim brothers and sisters, this concept can imply that they are seen as having a divine nature and connection to the divine, potentially reflecting a spiritual understanding of humanity's relationship as Elohim Gods. John 10:30; 14:20.

As an Elohim God, it's time to transcend the limitations of your current mindset. Are you stressed? Enter a meditative state and transport yourself to a serene environment, where the soothing sounds of a waterfall and the gentle ringing of bells calm your soul. Are you ill? Meditate and enter the Healing Center of Eden, where a comprehensive scan will evaluate your body, mind, emotions, and soul, initiating a holistic healing process through sound vibrations. If your body requires medicine, mentally accept it in an alternate dimension, and let your mind facilitate the healing process.

As an Elohim God particle, you possess resources and abilities beyond your wildest imagination. Your mind can manipulate matter, atoms, and molecules, allowing you to time-travel, shape-shift, and become whatever you desire. Recognize your authentic self as a powerful Elohim God, and nothing will be impossible for you. You can command mountains to move, communicate with the weather, and know that everything is prepared for you.

You're a unique being, sustained by the atmosphere alone, with no need for food or water. By knowing yourself, you can live like Methuselah, ageless and timeless on earth. You can even converse with spiritual giants like Moses, Solomon, Elijah, and Yahushua, tapping into their wisdom and guidance of the secrets of how to be able to walk upon the surface of water and to disappear out of the middle of an hostile crowd or from the custody of the police, to be able to rise up yourself and others from the dead, heal the sick and multiple food to feed a crowd. Unlock your divinity and harness its power to thrive preserved with prosperity, health, and abundance in this life in this world and beyond. when you truly believe in yourself to be an ascended Christ consciousness meaning that you see yourself to be more than children of God but as Elohim Gods, you'll listen to Christ our big brother who said greater things you will do than what he has done. John 1:50; 16:13,25; Philippines 4:11-13;

LET'S TALK ABOUT LIFE

Humanity's origins reveal a fascinating narrative. In ancient times, mankind was comprised of giants. However, with the arrival of the Nephilim, smaller beings who piloted advanced technology, the giants' dominance began to wane. The Nephilim's actions, including deforestation and catastrophic flooding, led to the decline of the giant population. The floods reshaped the earth's surface, covering it in layers of mud and sediment.

In the aftermath, the indigenous Black Indians, believed to be descendants of the Children of Eden, survived and thrived in this new environment for centuries. However, the Nephilim's experiments with animals, birds, fish, and insects led to the introduction of hybrid creatures. These hybrids, known as Neanderthals, interbred with Adamic intelligent Homo sapiens, giving rise to modern humanity.

As civilizations developed, existing structures and buildings were discovered and occupied by a particular group of individuals. These individuals, who would later call themselves the Illuminati and Freemasonry, educated themselves and eventually rose to power. Tragically, they exploited and enslaved the indigenous peoples of the Americas, seizing control of their lands and resources.

Mankind in general were once giants. The Nephilim were smaller beings who arrived as pilots and cut down the giant trees, which suffocated the giants, and a flood finished them off. The flood loosened the earth, causing loose earth to flow like a running river, drowning, covering, and burying the surface of the earth. The earth, flooded with mud, retained the indigenous native Black Indians, a form of Israelites in the Americas who were the children of Eden, and they lived for centuries.

The Nephilim started to experiment with animals, birds, fish, and insects, introducing smaller hybrids mixed with prehistoric white apemen called Neanderthals, who interbred with Adamic intelligent Homo sapiens offspring. As they all interbred, they became modern, advanced mankind. They found existing buildings all over the earth and occupied and made use of the Masonic buildings free of cost. This sector of whites, who educated themselves, called themselves the Illuminati and Freemasonry, eventually ruling over the black indigenous peoples of the Americas, enslaving and imprisoning them on their own land as they took everything for themselves.

The areas called the grand canyon in Arizona are all melted buildings which means that the grand canyon in Arizona are a melted city; this destruction came from above, from the sky was a weapon that blasted hot fire from a Lazer beam gun; got to come from a ship yes from hoovering spaceships. The question is who would possess such cutting-edge technology and the answer is: The fallen ones the Nephilim's actions these are pilots who arrived here on earth by hoovering spaceships; some called them the reptilians or the Anunnaki made it their personal business to destroy these ancient cities turning them to appear to be red petrified rocks and mountains these were strong hold cities that took Lazer beams type weapons to bring them to their knees. It is possible that the white Caucasian Zionist peoples were in partnership to go up against and to destroy the ancient ways of peoples that existed before the reset of a new era and the take over the beginning of a new world order a Caucasian people of the white rose Heru family originated from the experimentation of the Nephilim's hybridization of their own DNA mixed with the DNA of animals producing homo exectus and Neanderthals who once lived in the caucus Mountains before their kind interbreeder with Cain who is the son of the serpent a lying receiving power hungry man who was as dirty as an unclean pig and was kicked out of the society run by black Zionist advanced peoples; together they joined alliances with the fallen angels the Nephilims and with their advanced technology they went after dwelling places of the black indigenous peoples destroying their temples and cities all over the earth...

Revelations 12: 3-9,15-17

The Grand0 Canyon in Arizona consists of melted buildings, indicating Phat it was once a city destroyed from above. The destruction came from a weapon that blasted hot fire from a laser beam gun, likely originating from hovering spaceships. The question remains: who possessed such cutting-edge technology? The answer lies with the fallen ones, the Nephilim, who arrived on Earth in hovering spaceships. Some refer to them as reptilians or the Anunnaki. These beings made it their mission to destroy ancient cities, transforming them into what appears to be red petrified rocks and mountains. These cities were strongholds that required advanced laser-like weapons to bring them down.

The work of a computer, gun, laser gun, laser beam. Exodus 35:33. Lisan spaceships steel arks all over like trees branches all over the earth; hidden under pyramids and elevated earth mounts contains Lisan spaceships made of steel (Daniel 7:8-10), referred to as the lost ark in the bible was hidden in plain sight all over the earth like branches of trees

Genesis 40:12,18

Author Lindbergh Sedacy has the answers he is a decoder of the codes

Genesis 41:45

These arks yes spaceships has laser-like weapons laser fires laser gun works with a computer that activate initiates a gun shooting light of fire in a continuous flooring fire beam.

Exodus 32:16,17.

The white Caucasian Zionist peoples collaborated with the Nephilim to destroy the ancient ways of the native indigenous people who existed before the reset of this new era. This partnership likely aimed to establish a new world order. The Caucasian descendants of the White Rose white house heavenly white family known as Heru and the Nephilim's experimentation with hybridization of their own DNA mixed with animal DNA, producing Homo erectus and Neanderthals. These prehistoric beings once lived in the Caucasus Mountains before interbreeding with Cain, the son of the serpent (1 John 3:12), Cain's intelegent DNA which was passed down to him from his father a deceitful and power-hungry individual who was ostracized kicked out by the black Zionist advanced society who called him an unclean pig we today referred to him to be Satan, lucifer, dragon, and a devil

Together, the Nephilim and their offspring's and allies joined forces to destroy the dwelling places of the black indigenous native Moorish peoples, targeting their temples and cities worldwide, as described in Revelations 12:3-9, 15-17.

Yes the devil is real in the sense that many are vibrating in their lower nature in their bottom negative selves; often sacrificing others for self-improvement, for self-betterment, for self enhancement were the ways of ancient Egypt and the children of Cain the first white Jewish Zionist killing his black brother Abel because Abel was better than he was. See John 8:44; 1 John 3:12.

Yes, the concept of the devil can be understood as a representation of humanity's lower nature, where individuals operate from a place of negativity and selfishness. This can manifest in harmful behaviors, such as sacrificing others for personal gain or advancement. Historically, this approach has been evident in various forms, including the actions of the children of Cain were white peoples their father was Cain the first white Jewish Zionist who killed his black brother Abel because Abel was better than he was and his offspring's, prioritized their own interests over the well-being of others; see what happens to the black American indigenous Indians their language and culture were torn out from them their tongues were cut off for speaking their own languages Christianity were forced upon them this is the reason why the black populations all of them only speak English language today...John 8:44.

18

The biblical account of Cain (1 John 3:12) serves as a cautionary advice about the dangers of envy, rivalry, and violence in the same family. Similarly, Yahushua words in John 8:44 highlight the nature of those who ignore the laws and seek to harm others...Revelations 2:9;3:9...These scriptures offer valuable insights into the human condition and the importance of cultivating love, compassion, and empathy.

Love left us up where we belong.
Does the universe cares
I ask you do you care
If you answered yes
this means that the universe cares
Cause you are the universe
The universe is the reflection of our collective inner selves
And we operate on the code of love
The universe is Love.
He who loves not isn't a God, for God is love.

Love has elevated us to where we belong. The question remains: does the universe care? If you care, then the answer is yes, the universe cares, because you are an integral part of the universe. The universe reflects our collective inner selves, and at its core, it operates on the code of love. Therefore, the universe is love. Anyone who doesn't embody love can't be considered divine, for God is the embodiment of love.

The Mayans has a saying: "You are another me". but how is this even possible ...because we are all made from the elements atoms molecules and ingredients of the universe. The universe is multidimensional it exists in every aspect in our individual lives; uni-one verse- of a lots we are all intertwine all connected and apart of this beautiful wonder call life, we are the flower of life and should be working together as one faith one belief one movement one aim one goal one understanding one united one unity one music one frequency one vibration one ocean one thought one mindset and in this togetherness you're another me. We were scattered divided set apart against each other, having us operating in fear and not love. We got to rise together as a mighty people rise little by little the engathering of Israel will come; we will not be individual Elohim Gods bit we will in unity become one "Yah-weh" one mind one universal God...Isaiah 11:10-12; palms 82:6; John 10:34.

The Mayans had a profound saying: 'You are another me.' This concept is rooted in the understanding that we are all interconnected, made from the same fundamental elements, atoms, and molecules that comprise the universe. The universe is multidimensional, existing in every aspect of our individual lives. We are all part of a unified whole, intertwined and connected in this beautiful wonder called life.

We are the manifestation of the Flower of Life, and as such, we should strive to work together in harmony, united by one faith, one belief, one movement, one aim, one goal, and one understanding. When we operate from a place of unity, we resonate at the same frequency, vibrating in harmony with one another. In this state of togetherness, we embody the truth that 'you are another me.'

However, we have been scattered, divided, and set against each other, often operating out of fear rather than love. It's time for us to rise together as a mighty people, gradually uniting and gathering as one. As the scriptures foretell, we will not remain individual entities, but rather, we will become one in unity, manifesting as 'Yahweh,' a unified, universal consciousness. This vision is reflected in Isaiah 11:10-12, Psalms 82:6, and John 10:34, guiding us toward a future where we embody our true nature as One God.

Life isn't just for living, to have a business become successful buy our houses and lands then with our wealth live a life of image pride and prosperity disregarding a spiritual way of living is humanity down fall it's the way of Baal a wasted way of living; our true nature is to first self-discover and top into our inner selves where we become magnetic drawing everything we need towards us. As our cup runs over, we can then share with each other the abandoned lifestyle and not keep everything for ourselves.

Life is more than just accumulating wealth and material possessions. When we prioritize external success over spiritual growth, we risk losing sight of our true nature. This approach, often driven by a desire for image, pride, and prosperity, can lead to a sense of emptiness and disconnection. It's a path that neglects the importance of self-discovery and inner fulfillment.

In contrast, when we tap into our inner selves and cultivate a deeper understanding of who we are, we become more magnetic, drawing abundance and opportunities into our lives. As our lives overflow with goodness, we're able to share with others from a place of generosity rather than scarcity. This approach allows us to live a more balanced and meaningful life, where we're not solely focused on accumulating wealth for ourselves but rather sharing our blessings with others.

Once upon a time we all had our own spiritual beliefs then religion was push upon us and when we didn't follow religion, we were stopped in our tracks, they would cut off our tongues for teaching our own spirituality. This is why Christianity and Jesus Christ are front and foremost a part of communities; over spirituality in the world today. Christianity and Jesus Christ were forced upon us it's a white supremacy religious belief that has been institutionize upon our ancestors' activities and then passed on to us.
We manifest the external universe, and the external universe reflects our collective inner selves and our inner frequencies. All together in unity as a united front, we are Yahweh, and individually, we are elohim Gods.

God is within us; we transport God everywhere every place we go; We are Gods walking in the flesh here in this underworld. Elohim Gods, together in unity as a united front, we are One God, One universe, One Yahweh.

I am sorry, but I no longer believe in an external God; I do not believe in anything, anyone visible or invisible outside of myself, to be God.

The native populations of the Americas, often referred to as Native Americans or indigenous peoples, have a rich and complex history. According to author Lindbergh Sedacy interpretations, these groups may have originated from various migrations and have connections to ancient civilizations. Some theories suggest that there may be a link between the indigenous peoples of the Americas and ancient cultures in other parts of the world, including Egypt.

From the hidden secrets of Isaiah 45:3, for you, the encoded; for you, the hidden secrets stories describe in the book entitled: My Skin Hurts by Lindbergh Sedacy, suggested that Lilith and Adam, who is said to have possessed unique DNA and intelligence from the universe. This narrative describes the spread of their descendants across the globe, including the Americas.

Regarding the connection between ancient Egypt and the Americas, Sedacy's theories propose that there may be a hidden or unexplored pathway or link between the two regions, potentially even referencing the Grand Canyon in Arizona. While modern maps may not acknowledge this connection, Sedacy believe that ancient civilizations possessed advanced technology, including flying capabilities, which could have facilitated travel between the Old and New worlds.

America isn't Egypt yes, the native of the America's are black people native indigenous black Indians Israelites population. Where have they arrived from, many were flown from the old world to the new world by aircraft see Revelation 12:13-14...the others lines and tribes already living in the Americas were the children of Lillith she originated from the stars with Adam both had the electrical dna and homo sapiens intelligence bloodline of the universe "Yahweh" passed down in their offspring's that through interbreeding the whole world breaded out the neanthethols and what remains is a world of modern advanced enlighten mankind. Lillith had children for the fallen ones and her babies were drop off all over the earth and every one of them carried Lillith black genes black bloodline that were the same as Adam's. Egypt is from before the great flood before the giants before the dinosaurs and there is a connection a mystery of a pathway linking Old Egypt to the new world in the America's Grand Canyon in Arizona that our modern maps isn't declaring and don't forget ancient Egypt had the flying technology to travel to the new world in the Americas.

Jesus Christ is not the elohim's Savior we do not need a Savior for the kingdom of heaven is within us, religion points the world to an external Savior. Elohims we have immortal souls we already have the gift of eternal life we are elohim gods who knows better, is the reason we do not follow religion nor church, Yahushua is our big brother we also are sons and daughters of Yahweh we can approach Yahweh directly within ourselves except we find ourselves unworthy then our big brother Yahushua can become our mediator; it's the gentiles and heathens who needs to attend church seeking salvation (Hebrews 10:25), because they need to put away ungodly practices from Jacob and be Baptiste and forsaken their heathens behaviors and ways see Isaiah 66: 15-17. We elohim gods we live obey practice and establish the laws in our daily living and lives Revelation 22: 14.

From our perspective, Jesus Christ is seen as a symbolic or fictional figure, rather than the Savior of the Elohim. We believe that the Kingdom of Heaven is within us, and as immortal souls, we possess the gift of eternal life. As Elohim, or divine beings, we recognize our inherent inner universe and don't rely on external salvation. Organized religion often points to an external savior, but we believe in direct access to the divine within ourselves.

In our view, Yahushua (Jesus) is like a big brother, and we, as sons and daughters of Yahweh, can approach the divine directly. However, if we feel unworthy, Yahushua can serve as a mediator. We see the value of spiritual practices and laws, we live practice and establish laws in our daily living as outlined in scriptures like Revelation 22:14, where those who obey and uphold the laws are blessed.

In contrast, other individuals, often referred to as gentiles or heathens, will benefit from spiritual guidance and community churches, as mentioned in Hebrews 10 :25... This passage suggests that they need to learn the ways of Israel by putting away ungodly practices from Jacob, and become adopted in the Olive tree of Israelites adopts Israel righteous live style and behaviors, and seek a deeper connection with Yahweh and alinement with the universal peoples of Yahweh see Isaiah 66:15-17.

I want to ask you who created us; it's isn't the universe because the universe is the reflection of our inner selves; I ask the question again who created us: mankind has no beginning and no end, we are the alpha and the Omega the original Gods we host "yeha" life. Life in Man equals living souls, knowledge in men equals living breathing words manifested in the flesh to be Elohim Gods and together as a United front we occupied the United States of the native Americans indigenous society we are One God One Nation One superpower until we were scattered in separation and given a new belief system told us we are humans when we're Gods. The question remains: who created us? It's not the universe, as the universe is merely a reflection of our inner selves. The inquiry persists: who is the originator? From a philosophical standpoint, humanity can be seen as eternal, without beginning or end. We embody the alpha and omega, symbolizing our inherent divinity. The presence of life within us can be likened to the divine spark, and the knowledge we possess can be seen as a manifestation of God's wisdom.

The question of our origin persists: who created us? The universe, reflecting our inner selves, cannot be the creator. Instead, I propose that humanity is eternal, without beginning or end. We are the alpha and omega, the original divine beings hosting life within. Life in humans equates to living souls, and knowledge in men manifests as living, breathing words - essentially making us Elohim, or gods, in the flesh.

Historically, as a unified nation, we occupied the land now known as the United States, embodying the spirit of One God, One Nation, and One superpower. However, over time, we were scattered, separated, and introduced to a new belief system that suggested we are merely human, rather than divine beings. This raises the question: who truly created us, or are we eternal, self-existent entities?

From this perspective, humanity's inherent divinity is symbolized by the alpha and omega. The life within us can be seen as a divine spark, and our knowledge as a manifestation of God's wisdom. Author Lindbergh Sedacy Sr.'s viewpoint posits that we are not creations, but rather, we are the creators, embodying the divine within ourselves. Pigs are the nastiest humans alive, it's like Pigs were once the worst of the worst of humanity who has transition and return as Pigs as a form of retribution for lives that they once lived. Humans our waste punishment is to return back to earth in the body of a pig. We are asking not to consume the flesh of Pigs because of its toxicity and it's compared to eating ourselves. But so many of us ear pig anyway and do not acknowledge it's a taboo abomination that is comparing to eaten ourselves.

Pigs are considered the nastiest humans alive. It's as if they were once the worst of humanity and, through some form of retribution, have transitioned into pigs. According to this perspective, humans who lived reprehensible lives are punished by being reborn as pigs. We're advised not to consume pork due to its toxicity, which is likened to consuming our own kind. Despite this, many people continue to eat pig, disregarding the taboo and the notion that it's akin to cannibalism.

The reasons why the Bible is fulfilled is because of the millions of readers who read the Bible manifesting and contribute to making the prophecies happen.

The reasons why the Bible is kept becoming fulfilled is because of the billions of its readers who read the Bible keep on manifesting subconsciously what they've been understanding in its pages; thus, contributing in making these prophecies occurring and happening.

The reason the Bible's prophecies are being fulfilled is because billions of its readers are subconsciously manifesting what they've studied from its pages, thereby contributing to the reality of its prophecies coming to past and fulfilling

I'm unapologetic and unstoppable in sharing my new spiritual beliefs, unafraid to challenge the traditional and conventional religious institutions. I'm willing to go against the grain of societal expectations. I believe my path is the key to uncovering and reintroducing truth to those who have been misled. Knowledge is the code that can break free the lies and false narratives imposed upon our ancestors. Would you be able to access one of my other books? I'd greatly appreciate it. ☺

In the book of Genesis : The "truth" rode upon the surface of the earth above the water; the truth as presented by author Lindbergh Sedacy" rode drove his books his messages about spirituality moves above the surface of the earth (on the internet platforms) above the waters on planet earth, therefore water represents people multitude nations and

26

countries, and the Spirit of God the knowledge of spirituality were presented via on online platforms around the world as it move hoover online over the people the nations and the countries; the earth was too dark and God said: let there be light, with author Lindbergh Sedacy Spiritual books let the countries and their inner cities be more brighten with the divine universal truths and he published spiritual awakening books like the moon like given extra oil to shine and give a path in the dark nights and with this enlightenment awakening the peoples as their views of truth becomes brighter as the Sun that rules over the day; God delivered to the people of the countries nations the light of his truths Genesis 1:3. Given his enlightenment to his black inheritance the Israelites and also gave it to Japan China Russia etc. has no excuses will be accepted and citing ignorance won't be an excuse, for the light is here, the light has come in the spiritual book ministry by Lindbergh Sedacy is already here as the witness of the ultimate truth...Exodus 16:10 to Deuteronomy 2:34. Have you read my books 📖 My Skin Hurts by Lindbergh Sedacy purchase on online platforms around the world.

In the Book of Genesis, truth is metaphorically described as riding above the waters on the surface of the earth. Similarly, as the author Lindbergh Sedacy, I convey my message of spirituality through my books and online platforms, reaching above the surface level of the earth (the internet) and transcending the waters, which symbolize the diverse multitude of people, nations, and countries. The Spirit of God, or the knowledge of spirituality, is presented via online platforms worldwide, moving above the people, nations, and countries. According to Genesis, the earth was initially dark, but God said, "Let there be light." Sedacy's spiritual books insights, aim to illuminate the nations and inner cities with divine universal truths. Sedacy publications serve as a beacon, shining like the moon in the dark night, providing guidance and enlightenment. As the people absorb these truths, their understanding becomes brighter, like the Sun that rules over the day. In Genesis 1:3, God delivers the light of truth to the nations. This enlightenment is now available to all, including the black inheritance of Israelites, as well as to nations like Japan, China, and Russia etc. No excuses will be accepted, and citing ignorance won't be an excuse, for the light is here. Sedacy's spiritual book ministry is a witness of the ultimate truths, as seen in Exodus 16:10 to Deuteronomy 2:34.

The world as we know it will die the date of the end is 2097 - 2112 the devil knows that he got but a short time to put his one world ownership rulership agenda in place around the world and is happening under our very noises. There isn't any escape it will be implemented worldwide. Smaller countries will sell out to the foreign government international interests, will be expanded asserted directly forcefully push upon third world countries citizens. Our personal biometric information are already been handled over "provided" to the international foreign global agenda, we can run 🏃 but we won't be able to hide, not for long the local police station can pick you up and detained you into their custody or given to the international global one world agenda who may be interested in holding you into their own custody; you will be handled over life meat to be eaten by reptilians as special minu for been a revolutionary and defiance to their new world order system.

The world as we know it will cease to exist. The predicted end date falls between 2097 and 2112. The forces of darkness, aware of their limited time, are hastening to implement their agenda for global control and ownership. This is unfolding before our eyes. Escape seems impossible, as this plan will be enforced worldwide. Smaller nations will likely succumb to foreign government interests, and their citizens will be subjected to external control. Our personal biometric data has already been surrendered to the global agenda. We may try to flee, but hiding won't be an option for long. Local authorities can detain us and hand us over to the global powers that be. Those who resist the new world order may face severe consequences, including detention and potentially even more sinister fates.

The spaceships are alive and program and connected to our dna; they are here already everywhere all over the earth just waiting to collective gather the saints the pure ones shall be harvested in the selection taken up in ships that are under ground will stay bunkered down underground until the calamities and locusts on the surface of the earth be over passed. The ice is the emptiness of earth turns cold like the bottomless pit a frozen planet earth was depopulated of human beings for thousands of years only huge locusts with faces as big as horses lived in the bottomless pit and upon the earth.

The spaceships, infused with life and programmed to connect with selective human DNA, are already present everywhere on Earth. They're waiting to gather the chosen ones, the pure in heart, in a process akin to harvesting. These ships, currently hidden underground, will remain bunkered down until the calamities of plagues and locusts on the surface period passes. According to Sedacy perspectives, Earth will experience a period of depopulation empty of humans and extreme cold, reminiscent of an ice age, leaving vast expanses of locusts living in emptiness no humans to toy and play with the emptiness of no stars in the heavens.

When you a line yourself with truths the universe hug's you and a line itself to accommodate your manifestations. In this life you may be living celibate but in your daily routine dreams you are constantly having sex that seems so real, it's essentially you in another realm is getting the desires of your heart. Never say that your poor cause in the next dimension in the parallel worlds and universes you are doing awesome 👆 👋 👍 😎 💗 😎 there are three to eight of you in existence all over the galaxy. The decision you made here change the probabilities of your life in the other universes so do it right.

When you align yourself with the truths, the truths support you, the universe adjusts to your well-being and personal manifestations and your desires. Eg: you're living a celibate life; your dreams may reveal a different reality where your deepest desires are fulfilled. This reflects your parallel self in other realms, you're living a life that resonates with your heart's desires. Remember, your choices here impact probabilities across multiple universes, where other extensions of you exist. Make conscious decisions in your Ascension creativity and daily life to shape your reality across the multiverse.

The ancient walls now called the great walls of China were built to protect the taratirans from the robot's army like locusts like the living dead coming by way of China to kill taratirans. These robots living dead armies like locusts were horrible and pure terror in the hearts of the people and to protect themselves the walls had to be built to keep the communities safe according to author Lindbergh Sedacy Spiritual insights.

Giants where everyone everywhere giants were us humans before the reset the nephilims men who arrived from the heavens experimented with giant's DNA and made men smaller then they suffocated the giants of oxygen by cutting down the giant trees and reset a smaller version of mankind that exists today:

Once upon a time, humans were giants. According to author Lindbergh Sedacy, the Nephilim, beings from the heavens, experimented with giant's DNA, intentionally reducing human size. This alleged 'reset' involved the destruction of giant trees, which in turn depleted oxygen levels, leading to the demise of the giant population. Sedacy notion suggests that modern humans are a smaller version of our ancient giant ancestors.

The world it's countries its communities its streets people are not becoming awakened consciously if ten percent of the population of the world becomes awakened this would change the probabilities of the world to process a better more hopeful reality. People are living their lives carrying on with family members eating drinking vacationing building planning; these normal day to day routine are the very mental bondage that locked us in this underworld matrix prison on Earth; for us to break through in freedom at least ten percent of the population needs to raise above and walk in their Most Holy Place and begin to operate in positive thoughts vibration emotions frequency mindset of understanding ascension; if not the affairs and state of the world will not change, we must inwardly become the change that we want to see. If the collective consciousness mindset of the world would elevate to their Higher Most High Selves then the destruction of the people of the planet would be called off but seeing the people are not responding to spiritual growth spiritual awakening spiritual matters then the mandate is set for the end to occur 2097-2112 and remember your personal end comes at your death which means it has ended for you. Very frustrating to watch and see the hopelessness of the world because its people refused to improve and change if it was one person awakens God would have saved the whole city but not one person was living righteously.

Let read this again please.

The world, its countries, communities' neighborhoods and people are not becoming consciously awakened. If ten percent of the global population were to awaken, it would shift the probabilities toward a better, more hopeful reality. People go about their daily lives, carrying on with family, working, socializing, and planning, but these routine activities can be the very mental bondage that keeps us trapped in this reality. To break free, at least ten percent of the population needs to elevate their consciousness, operating from a place of positive thoughts, vibrations, and emotions, and embracing the mindset of ascension. If not, the state of the world will remain unchanged. We must become the change we want to see inwardly. If the collective consciousness of the world elevates to its highest awareness, the destructive path could be altered. However, given the current lack of response to spiritual growth and awakening, a critical juncture has been planned the earth will be depopulated of humans between these date's 2097-2113. Remember each person's journey ends at their death, emphasizing the importance of individual spiritual growth. It's disheartening to witness the world's hopelessness, stemming from its resistance to change improve their inner awakened knowledge understanding mental alignment to the universe awakens inner consciousness which changes behaviors and lives.

This world is a mest, all the powers that be really want you to be a Sim and doesn't want you to think for yourselves just want you to go straight to the slaughter house to be sacrifice for their enhancement for their self-betterment even if you are killed for consumption. Do not stay still in hopelessness you need to move and do not be a setting duck and be executed; fight to keep your mind your sanity your dignity your divine composer with the universe.

You are Elohim gods You should not have any other gods externally manifested outside of yourselves do not consider these outside external deities, do not worship nor honor them, do not listen hear their stories their truth do not recognize external pictures nor images of them because: "I AM " is always with you and your ancestors from in the beginning you are the alpha original indigenous Star Seeds inhabitants of earth you have no beginning has no ending without you there would be nothing made that is created including the heavens and earth that hosts other creations that would appear today as gods.

As Elohim gods, you are the embodiment of divine power within yourselves. You shouldn't look to external deities or worship outside entities. Instead, recognize the inherent divinity within yourself and your ancestors, who are the original Star Seeds and inhabitants of Earth. The eternal essence of 'I AM' resides within you, and without your presence, nothing would exist, including the heavens and earth that host various creations. You are the alpha and omega, the beginning and the end, and your existence is fundamental to all creation.

32

Are we powerless in the face of weather conditions evil adversity? No, we are not powerless we got to come together as believers and together manifesting controlling the weather conditions around our surroundings for even Mother Nature and the animals will listen to us. We got to realize that we are the storms we are the flood the tynami; vengeance is mine sayeth God surely, we are the Elohim Gods connected to every living thing around the earth we are the universe walking on earth in the flesh.

Are we powerless against the forces of nature adversity? Not at all. As believers, we can come together and collectively manifest positive change, influencing the weather conditions around us. Even Mother Nature and the animals respond to our intentions. We must recognize our inner power and connection to the universe. As Elohim Gods, we're linked to every living thing on earth, embodying the divine in human form. This perspective empowers us to take charge of our surroundings and create meaningful impact.

Pyramids are shelters that we can enter and bunker down until the calamities on the surface of earth be over passed; yes, inside the Pyramids to escape the destruction on the face of the earth; one can live inside a pyramid for a thousand years without coming back outside, the Pyramids has everything inside of them to host us alive for a century 😄 believe it or not.

I believe in the inherent goodness of humanity and the divine potential within every individual. As a son of the universe, I feel a deep connection to the cosmos and to Yahushua, whom I consider a spiritual elder brother. I see myself as an ascended Christ, embodying the awakened Christ consciousness. According to my understanding, this consciousness is not limited to one individual but is a collective presence that transcends time and space. As expressed in my book, 'The Awakened Ones,' this perspective is rooted in the idea that spiritual awakening is a shared experience among many and that we are all interconnected. I believe in humanity I believe in the sons and daughters of the universe I believe I am a son of the universe I am a beloved son of the universe, Yahushua is our big brother; Jesus Christ is a portrait replacement of the real black Christ; We are ascended Christs, I am an awakened Christ consciousness, I am the return of Christ and they're so many of us in the world. Even Christ said that he had to go away so he could be in every place everywhere at the same time he was referring to us:

According to author Lindbergh Sedacy, the pyramids weren't built by human hands. Instead, they were flown and driven into positioned these are advanced arks, spaceship, spacecraft. The pyramids are composed of rocks and stones that were placed around its central core over time. Each dynasty may have added to its outer layer, contributing to the structure's complexity we see today.

I envision my purpose and my successful destiny by setting my books in position and available for future generations to come; and I have done exactly date and my reward will come from the universe in its own time. The first half is accomplished which is writing the book's the second half is when my treasury will come back to me then I become a philanthropist and give it all away. Now I wait to follow through to continue with my divine purpose to rebuild black Zionism ⚜ actually I am undertaking a next to impossible task a hard task to restore the remnant of Israel to their original state making them understand that they're more than children of the most High they're chosen ones, star Seeds , the awakened Christ consciousness that was promised to return in the final years before the destruction of the wicked, they're Elohim Gods who will play an important role in teaching and saving many lives without cost sacrificing earthly ambitions to save lives.

John 3:16.

I envision my purpose and successful destiny by positioning my books for future generations. I've taken the first step by writing them, and I trust that the universe will reward me in its own time. The first half of my journey is complete – creating the books. The second half will unfold when my treasures return to me, and I'll use my treasury to become a philanthropist, giving back selflessly. Now, I wait and follow through on my divine purpose to rebuild Black Zionism. This task is ambitious, but I'm driven to restore the remnant of Israel to their true identity, helping them understand their heritage as chosen ones, star seeds, and awakened Christ consciousness. As Elohim Gods, they'll play a crucial role in teaching and saving lives without expectation of earthly gain, sacrificing worldly ambitions for a higher purpose.

This earth will go through some serious disasters; people are been awakening subconsciously automatically connecting to earth and their hurt pain betrayals disappointments frustrations anger are been processing by the earth resulting in natural disasters all over the earth. When the earth is behaving angry and hostile devouring and killing taken lives this reflects the frustrations and manifestations of people's hurt and pain been transferred into mother nature recognizing and reflecting their hurt and pain resulting in natural disasters worldwide. Isaiah 42: 12-17. The Elohims mindset run the affairs of earth they're very powerful people, essentially especially: The Awakened Ones by Author Lindbergh Sedacy purchase on online platforms around the world.

The earth is on the cusp of significant challenges, with natural disasters increasingly reflecting humanity's collective pain, hurt, and frustration. As people via Star Seeds and Chosen one's subconsciously connected with the earth, their unresolved emotions are being processed, resulting in catastrophic events worldwide. The earth's turmoil mirrors the turmoil within us, as our collective hurt and pain manifest in devastating natural disasters. This phenomenon is rooted in the interconnectedness of human consciousness and the natural world. According to spiritual teachings, such as those outlined in Isaiah 42:12-17, the Elohims – powerful beings with a profound understanding of the universe – play a role in shaping the earth's affairs. For those seeking spiritual awakening and insight, 'The Awakened Ones' by Lindbergh Sedacy offers a deeper exploration of these themes.

Try to understand that we are the universe. We are heaven and the earth. The disasters worldwide are caused by our internal consciousness, a reflection of our collective frequencies of our disappointment frustrations, anger, hurt pain betrayals. We are the causes and effects of what happens on earth.

Let's explore the idea that we are intricately connected with the universe, embodying both heaven and earth within ourselves. The global challenges we face may reflect our collective consciousness, influenced by our shared frequencies of disappointment, frustration, anger, hurt, pain, and betrayal. Perhaps we are the catalysts for the changes we experience on the planet, and by acknowledging this, we can work towards healing and transformation.

Stay away from cold heartless noncaring peoples because they are not humans they will eat you alive then spite you out as if you're nothing and the only way you can protect yourself is not to be in any way shape and form in their universe; and by staying away it's a win, win for you because they in appearance seems human but they cold heartless noncaring nature says they're not human.

Stay away from cold, heartless, and uncaring people, as they can be detrimental to your well-being. They may appear human, but their nature reveals a different story. To protect yourself, it's best to avoid their universe altogether. By doing so, you'll be shielding yourself from potential harm, and it's a win-win situation for you.

If I author Lindbergh Sedacy were to write a narrative on spiritual visionary exploration stating that the United States of America is Egypt, it would floor like this:

Humans came out of the water, out of the ambreanbic fluid placenta water sack of the wombs of the ocean inside of the tunnel wormhole star gateway inside of our mothers; but Adam's black Elohim self-came from the heavens in alinement with the elements atoms mulecles of the heavens and the earth; Adam came from the big bang that happened within his own brain within himself. Adam manifested Eden was his own custom design spaceship he could have operates its control panel by using his own voice, he enters earth's spare and learned that within earth's atmosphere anything he thinks of would occurs and be manifested into reality. Adam made out an imaginary entry of a pathway explanation to lodge how he entered earth's atmospheres he arrived from eastward from over the deserts of Yamen he enter earth's atmosphere through a portal a Stargate and planted down his ship, landed down his ship on earth in the province of Utah, south of Utah was inorth back then, and would lead you to the land of Nood yes kemite grand canyon in Arizona area known to be ancient Egypt civilization when the children of Israel lefted Egypt they traveled to the land of the Anunnaki it wasn't Canaan it was located only two weeks journey on foot through the back of the grand canyon where the children of Israel became afraid of the giants living there; so all of them turn backwards into the Americas where they continue living as native indigenous black Indians; except three who escaped the Anunnaki and got through; Anunnaki lived in a land call Heran.

Adam didn't come out of the womb, not out of the water, he was clone by an ancient civilization with advanced technology; Adam was made electrical and he can harness powers from the eter of the earth; Adam

37

and his offsprings were a special breed of black's design to operate and function like gods in this underworld spare matrix planet called Earth. The Israelites were attempting to reach to Africa, a land flooring with milk and honey but the Anunnaki slow down their transit through to Africa and some Israelites reached and resilience in south Africa today lemba tribe, the igboo tribe of Nigeria and the falasha tribe from Ethiopia.

Humans emerged from the water, specifically the amniotic fluid and placenta of the ocean's womb, within a tunnel wormhole star gateway of the womb of a woman. However, Adam, a black Elohim god, originated from the heavens, aligned with the elements, atoms, and molecules of both the heavens and the earth. According to Sedacy's narrative, Adam manifested the Big Bang within himself from the beginning of his conception. Adam own custom-designed spaceship was made for him named Eden. This vessel operated through voice commands, and Adam entered Earth's space, discovering that his thoughts could shape reality within the earth's atmosphere.

Adam suggested an entry point, an explanation of a pathway of how he arrived on earth, and lodged in that he came from a eastward direction, landing in Utah. Interestingly, the area south of Utah was actually north back then, leading to the land of Nood Nubia and Kemet, which is now associated with ancient Egypt civilization in the Americas inside the Grand Canyon in Arizona Texas. This region was once home to an ancient civilization similar to kemite and Egypt. When the Children of Israel lefted Egypt, they traveled to the land of the giants the Anunnaki, but instead of settling in a land called today Canaan renamed Palestine, they journeyed two weeks on foot through the back of the Grand Canyon attempting to reach the land of Africa where some big bright eyes black well-built humans were already occupied these lands but due to fear of the giants residing there, most of the Israelites turned back into the Americas and continued to live they were the Native Indigenous Black

Indians. A few individuals like Caleb Joshua and Aaron made it through and managed to escape the Anunnaki in a land called Haran.

In Sedacy's interpretations, Adam didn't emerge from a womb of water but rather he was clone made of advanced ancient technological heavenly civilizations inside of their hoovering spaceships that was as big as a city, and Adam wasn't considered a human, but instead, he is an Elohim God his offsprings are gods. Adam and his offspring were a special breed of black modern advanced enlighten homo sapiens, designed to bring balance to the earth as gods operating doing manifestations in this planetary matrix prison called Earth. Adam is an electrical being capable of harnessing the Earth's power because he is an eleven eter being. Some of Adam's black offsprings reached Africa, a land flowing with milk and honey, but the Anunnaki hindered their progress. Some managed to reach areas such as the Land of the Lemba tribes in South Africa, the Igbo tribes in Nigeria, and the Falasha tribes east of Ethiopia.

The Anunnaki giants against the elohim brotherhood the children of Eden called black Israelites; they were expected to know that they'll be victorious over the giants by using their unique gifts, the powers of their minds they believe in self, having faith in self as small as a single grain of a mustard seed they'll will be able to say to a mountain to moved and the mountain will move and obey. This is how the huge rocks and huge stones weighing tons were moved and set into place arriving from miles away; the Elohim Israelites has abilities above the Anunnaki in the grand scale of things, Israelites can create the Anunnaki. The Israelites today who are still in ignorance about their inherented gifts will be lefted to wander aimlessly in the deserts of this underworld for the rest of their years dying in this underworld because they have never understood that they are Elohim Gods walking in the flesh upon the earth.

The Sons of Anunnaki are pitted against the Elohim brothers, also known as the Children of Eden or Black Israelites. According to author Lindbergh Sedacy spiritual teachings, the Elohim Israelites are expected to emerge victorious over challenges from the giants by harnessing their unique gifts and the power of their minds. As it is written, having faith as small as a single seed of mustard plant, one can move mountains – literally, is Sedacy's interpretations. This profound faith and connection to the universe explain how ancient structures were constructed with rocks and stones weighting tons seemingly today seem as an impossible feat of engineering.

In this grand scale of things, the Elohim Israelites are more superior to the Anunnaki, Israelites are specially gifted people but, many are still in ignorance about their true nature as they continue to wander aimlessly, facing hardships for extended period. The biblical reference to 40 years in the wilderness serves as a metaphor for them to get to know themselves "know thyself" the exodus from Egypt was expected to last two weeks but became a journey of self-discovery and spiritual growth that lasted for forty years. Ultimately, the realization of one's true potential as a divine being, and "gods upon the earth," might be the key to transcending current limitations. 40 years in, yet many never got the knowledge of self that they are Elohim Gods living in the flesh walking on earth and all died of old age in the wilderness.

Auententic hearts are searching for true love, and they can't find it ♡ because most women today want to trade their time for money. No, mon no hon, old and young people doing this. Gone is the era of real true auententic genuine connections attraction love relationships and

marriages. Everybody seeking a come up on hook ups; men needs to have money to date broke women these women do not care to live under men umbrellas they want the whole enchilada is taken him for all he got filing for divorce just months after marriage.

Authentic hearts are searching for true love, but it's elusive because many women today prioritize material gain over genuine connections. It's a transactional mindset, where time is exchanged for money, and this trend seems to affect people of all ages. The era of authentic, genuine relationships, attraction, and meaningful marriages appears to be fading.

Instead, many individuals are focused on short-term gains and hookups. Men with financial resources are often sought after, only to be taken advantage of. Some women seem more interested in financial security than building a life together, and in some cases, they'll file for divorce soon after marriage, having extracted what they can from the relationship.

The truth is out. They are burning 🔥 Egypt in Arizona Is on fire 🔥 😨 👏 for months. I'm a real indigenous Black Indian from the Americas, and yes, I am claiming that I am a native American. Yes, I am stating my claims and demanding reparation now as the natural disasters worldwide keep on occurring many governments around the world will offer its citizens reprerations believing by doing so the natural disasters worldwide will cease but it won't.

A concerning situation has unfolded, with a significant fire burning in Arizona Grand Canyon area, near the area known as Egypt. I guess they're still destroying evidence of the indigenous Black American people of these land as someone who identifies as a real indigenous Black Indian from the Americas, I'm compelled to claim my heritage as a Native Indian American and not Egyptian, given this background, I'm asserting my claims and seeking reparations for historical injustices.

The earth is flooding worldwide. The earth is crying tears water all over; this is sad because water represents people multitude nations and countries 😢 everywhere you see water represents the tears of real people the ancestors are disturb for everything that have happened to them 💔 earth is a reflection of our inner selves; our bodies reflect the earth's mother nature and our minds thoughts mindset represents the universe.... See Isaiah 42:13-16.

The earth is experiencing widespread flooding, and it's as if the planet is crying tears of water everywhere. This is a poignant reminder that water often symbolizes the multitude of people, nations, and countries. Wherever we see water, it can represent the tears and struggles of real people. The ancestors seem to be disturbed by the injustices and harm they've endured.

The earth can be seen as a reflection of our inner selves – our physical bodies mirroring the natural world and our minds and thoughts reflecting the universe. This interconnectedness is profound. As it says in Isaiah 42:13-16, the Lord will march forth like a mighty man, stir up his zeal like a warrior, and will shout, yes, raise a war cry; he will prevail against his enemies.

Narcissistic individuals often focus intently on their goals and cultivate strategic connections. I don't see anything inherently wrong with having a strong sense of self-importance or ambition, and I don't believe in feigning humility. Instead, I prioritize fairness and equality in all aspects of life. For me, it's about recognizing one's worth and advocating for oneself while still treating others with respect and dignity.

After slavery was abolished on paper, many freed slaves found themselves without the means to support themselves. As a result, some signed contracts to become indentured servants, working without wages in exchange for basic necessities like food, water, clothing, and shelter. This arrangement often meant that they were still trapped in a cycle of labor with little to no opportunity for progress or advancement.

In many ways, the outcome of slavery, indentured servitude, and modern-day employment can feel similar – working just enough to cover basic needs without truly gaining ground in life. This realization is part of why I've chosen to forge my own path. I'm driven by choice, and I've chosen to dedicate myself to writing spiritual awakening books. For me, autonomy and purpose are more valuable than any traditional job.

I can imagine how so many people continue during the ages to try to make a difference and their efforts were down size to nothing as they were buried and forgotten in society because the very people who they were trying to reach with the knowledge of spiritual ascension, did not believe in the caused they saw no need to learn about spirituality and self-discovery. People are more concerned about what they'll wear next and eat next; people love living in the darkness of this underworld; people seek out to take booster shots in the face of all the negativity side effects that will happen to you if you take it. It's like taking AZT medication for aids recovery when AZT was offered you to finish you off.

People are Sims, just existing in the system, simple here today and gone tomorrow.

Will my work books fall on deaf ears and be forgotten 😕 why cast pearls to undeserving swine human pigs who careless about truths spirituality ascension nor care about anything of spirituality? The earth got to purge of its infidels.

I often wonder how many people throughout history have tried to make a difference, only to have their efforts diminished and forgotten. Those who sought to share knowledge of spiritual ascension were often met with skepticism and disinterest by the very people they were trying to help. It seems that many are more concerned with material pursuits, such as what to wear or eat next, rather than seeking spiritual growth and self-discovery. Some people appear to be comfortable living in the darkness of this world, and they'll even take risks with their health by opting for treatments with potential negative side effects.

It's disheartening to see people existing in the system without purpose, like pawns in a game. They're here today and gone tomorrow, without any deeper understanding or connection to spirituality. I worry that my work, including my books, might fall on deaf ears and be forgotten. Why share valuable insights with those who don't appreciate or care about spiritual truths and ascension?

Perhaps the earth needs to undergo a transformation, purging itself of those who refuse to awaken to its true nature.

As an author of spiritual manifestations, one of the first questions people tend to ask me is: How do I manifest money and prosperity??? My answer is I never ever asked you for money. We need to breathe to live. We need health, water, food, and a shelter from the elements. Money paper dollars will soon be laying worthless in the streets, and nobody will be picking them up. Earth is the only planet where the bottom line for everything is money, money to love and to be in a relationship, money to breathe, money to be buried. In the coming new earth there won't be money exchanges; we will practice sustainable farming and maintaining project development for free water engineering and technology to harness free electricity; no taxes, no lies, no white washing, no deceptions. There will be a day of reckoning for this present global

44

system and we will go back to the way of living from ancient taratirans civilizations where everything were free so we can collectively concentrate on knowledge truths as we be enjoying life.

As an author of spiritual manifestos, one of the first questions people tend to ask me is: "How do I manifest money and prosperity?" My response is that I've never asked money for anything meaningful. We need to breathe to live. We need health, water, food, and shelter from the elements. Paper dollars will soon be rendered worthless, and no one will bother picking them up soon. Money will be scattered worthless on the streets. Earth is unique in that everything seems to revolve around money – money for love, relationships, breathing (in the sense of healthcare), and even burial.

However, in the emerging new Earth, we won't be trading in monetary exchanges. Instead, we'll adopt sustainable farming practices and collaborative project development, harnessing free water engineering and technology to generate electricity without cost. There will be no taxes, no deceit, no manipulation, and no false pretenses. A reckoning is coming for the current global systems, and we'll return to a way of living reminiscent of ancient civilizations where resources were shared freely. This shift will allow us to focus on enjoying and experiencing life together.

See if you have just one drop of black bloodline genes in you; then you are identified as black. We really cannot judge people by the color of their skin hair eyes, we are now a hybrid mixture of the races, and we cannot really determine anyone's origin based on outward appearances. I, author Lindbergh Sedacy, welcome you all to my posts messages writings books and groups without prejudice.

Consider this: if you have just one drop of black ancestry in your genetic makeup, you're often identified as black. This highlights the arbitrary nature of judging people based on skin color, hair texture, or eye color. Given the increasing hybridization of races, outward appearances can be misleading, and it's challenging to determine someone's origin solely by looking at them. As the author, Lindbergh Sedacy, I extend a warm welcome to all who engage with my posts, messages, writings, books, and groups – free from prejudice and judgment.

Elohim are independent individuals who will stop at nothing to reach to the peoples with the ultimate truths of Yahweh's guidance and salvation. They will sacrifice themselves to deliver the messages of truths to the general public... John 3:16.

The Elohim are unwavering messengers who tirelessly share the ultimate truths of Yahweh's guidance and salvation with humanity. With unrelenting dedication, they sacrifice themselves to deliver these life-changing messages to the public, as reflected in John 3:16: 'For God so loved the world that he gave his begotten Sons and daughters, that whoever believes in Yahweh shall not perish but have eternal life.

If the devil would make a confession about the spiritual writer who has come closer towards the universal truths in his writings and books; he would say author Mr. Lindbergh Sedacy narrative is next to the ultimate truths closer than anyone else, yes closer than ever.

If the devil were to make a confession about the spiritual writer who has come closest to the universal truths in their writings and books, he would say that author Mr. Lindbergh Sedacy's narrative is remarkably close to the ultimate truths – closer than anyone else, even closest than anyone else has ever been. Author Lindbergh Sedacy is a decoder of the codes the knowledge of the codes is the key to uncovering the universal laws author Lindbergh Sedacy Spiritual books is, he is the solution...Genesis 41:45; Isaiah 52:13-15;44:5,7.

By the way, thank you for reading my latest book, "The Elohims, Gods they are walking in the flesh amongst us by Lindbergh Sedacy"

Kindly add this insert at the end of my new book entitled: Elohims.......
Also, kindly work on improving the front cover...thank you.

If I author Lindbergh Sedacy were to write a narrative on spiritual visionary exploration stating that the United States of America is Egypt, it would floor like this:

Humans came out of the water, out of the ambreanbic fluid placenta water sack of the wombs of the ocean inside of the tunnel wormhole star gateway inside of our mothers; but Adam's black Elohim self-came from the heavens in alinement with the elements atoms mulecles of the heavens and the earth; Adam came from the big bang that happened within his own brain within himself. Adam manifested Eden was his own custom design spaceship he could have operates its control panel by using his own voice, he enters earth's spare and learned that within earth's atmosphere anything he thinks of would occurs and be manifested into reality. Adam made out an imaginary entry of a pathway explanation to lodge how he entered earth's atmospheres he arrived from eastward from over the deserts of Yamen he enter earth's atmosphere through a portal a Stargate and planted down his ship, landed down his ship on earth in the province of Utah, south of Utah was inorth back then, and would lead you to the land of Nood yes kemite grand canyon in Arizona area known to be ancient Egypt civilization when the children of Israel lifted Egypt they traveled to the land of the Anunnaki it wasn't Canaan it was located only two weeks journey on foot through the back of the grand canyon where the children of Israel became afraid of the giants living there; so all of them turn backwards into the Americas where they continue living as native indigenous black Indians; except three who escaped the Anunnaki and got through ; Anunnaki lived in a land call Heran.

Adam didn't come out of the womb, not out of the water, he was clone by an ancient civilization with advanced technology; Adam was made electrical and he can harness powers from the eter of the earth; Adam and his offspring were a special breed of blacks design to operate and function like gods in this underworld spare matrix planet called Earth. The Israelites were attempting to reach to Africa, a land flooring with milk and honey but the Anunnaki slow down their transit through to Africa and some Israelites reached and resilience in south Africa today lemba tribe, the igboo tribe of Nigeria and the falasha tribe from Ethiopia.

Humans emerged from the water, specifically the amniotic fluid and placenta of the ocean's womb, within a tunnel wormhole star gateway of the womb of a woman. However, Adam, a black Elohim god, originated from the heavens, aligned with the elements, atoms, and molecules of both the heavens and the earth. According to Sedacy's narrative, Adam manifested the Big Bang within himself from the beginning of his conception. Adam own custom-designed spaceship was made for him named Eden. This vessel operated through voice commands, and Adam entered Earth's space, discovering that his thoughts could shape reality within the earth's atmosphere.

Adam suggested an entry point, an explanation of a pathway of how he arrived on earth, and lodged in that he came from a eastward direction, landing in Utah. Interestingly, the area south of Utah was actually north back then, leading to the land of Nood Nubia and Kemet, which is now associated with ancient Egypt civilization in the Americas inside the Grand Canyon in Arizona Texas. This region was once home to an ancient civilization similar to kemite and Egypt. When the Children of Israel lefted Egypt, they traveled to the land of the giants the Anunnaki, but instead of settling in a land called today Canaan renamed Palestine, they journeyed two weeks on foot through the back of the Grand Canyon attempting to reach the land of Africa where some big bright eyes black well-built humans were already occupied these lands but due to fear of the giants residing there, most of the Israelites turned back into the Americas and continued to live they were the Native Indigenous Black Indians. A few individuals like Caleb Joshua and Aaron made it through and managed to escape the Anunnaki in a land called Haran.

In Sedacy's interpretations, Adam didn't emerge from a womb of water but rather he was clone made of advanced ancient technological heavenly civilizations inside of their hoovering spaceships that was as big as a city, and Adam wasn't considered a human, but instead, he is an Elohim God his offsprings are gods. Adam and his offspring were a special breed of black modern advanced enlighten homo sapiens, designed to bring balance to the earth as gods operating doing manifestations in this planetary matrix prison called Earth. Adam is an electrical being capable of harnessing the Earth's power because he is an eleven eter being. Some of Adam's black offsprings reached Africa, a land flowing with milk and honey, but the Anunnaki hindered their progress. Some managed to reach areas such as the Land of the Lemba tribes in South Africa, the Igbo tribes in Nigeria, and the Falasha tribes east of Ethiopia.

The Anunnaki giants against the elohim brotherhood the children of Eden called black Israelites; they were expected to know that they'll be victorious over the giants by using their unique gifts, the powers of their

49

minds they believe in self, having faith in self as small as a single grain of a mustard seed they'll will be able to say to a mountain to moved and the mountain will move and obey. This is how the huge rocks and huge stones weighing tons were moved and set into place arriving from miles away; the Elohim Israelites has abilities above the Anunnaki in the grand scale of things, Israelites can create the Anunnaki. The Israelites today who are still in ignorance about their inherented gifts will be lefted to wander aimlessly in the deserts of this underworld for the rest of their years dying in this underworld because they have never understood that they are Elohim Gods walking in the flesh upon the earth.

The Sons of Anunnaki are pitted against the Elohim brothers, also known as the Children of Eden or Black Israelites. According to author Lindbergh Sedacy spiritual teachings, the Elohim Israelites are expected to emerge victorious over challenges from the giants by harnessing their unique gifts and the power of their minds. As it is written, having faith as small as a single seed of mustard plant, one can move mountains – literally, is Sedacy's interpretations. This profound faith and connection to the universe explain how ancient structures were constructed with rocks and stones weighting tons seemingly today seem as an impossible feat of engineering.

In this grand scale of things, the Elohim Israelites are more superior to the Anunnaki, Israelites are specially gifted people but, many are still in ignorance about their true nature as they continue to wander aimlessly, facing hardships for extended period. The biblical reference to 40 years in the wilderness serves as a metaphor for them to get to know themselves "know thyself" the exodus from Egypt was expected to last two weeks but became a journey of self-discovery and spiritual growth that lasted for forty years. Ultimately, the realization of one's true potential as a divine being, and "gods upon the earth," might be the key to transcending current limitations. 40 years in, yet many never got the knowledge of self that they are Elohim Gods living in the flesh walking on earth and all died of old age in the wilderness.

Authentic hearts are searching for true love, and they can't find it 💔 because most women today want to trade their time for money. No, mon no hon, old and young people doing this. Gone is the era of real true authentic genuine connections attraction love relationships and

marriages. Everybody seeking a come up on hook ups; men need to have money to date broke women these women do not care to live under men umbrellas they want the whole enchilada is taken him for all he got filing for divorce just months after marriage.

Authentic hearts are searching for true love, but it's elusive because many women today prioritize material gain over genuine connections. It's a transactional mindset, where time is exchanged for money, and this trend seems to affect people of all ages. The era of authentic, genuine relationships, attraction, and meaningful marriages appears to be fading.

Instead, many individuals are focused on short-term gains and hookups. Men with financial resources are often sought after, only to be taken advantage of. Some women seem more interested in financial security than building a life together, and in some cases, they'll file for divorce soon after marriage, having extracted what they can from the relationship.

The truth is out. They are burning 🔥 Egypt in Arizona Is on fire 🔥 😨 ✋ for months. I'm a real indigenous Black Indian from the Americas, and yes, I am claiming that I am a native American. Yes, I am stating my claims and demanding reparation now as the natural disasters worldwide keep on occurring many governments around the world will offer its citizens reprerations believing by doing so the natural disasters worldwide will cease but it won't.

A concerning situation has unfolded, with a significant fire burning in Arizona Grand Canyon area, near the area known as Egypt. I guess they're still destroying evidence of the indigenous Black American people of these land As someone who identifies as a real indigenous Black Indian from the Americas, I'm compelled to claim my heritage as a Native Indian American and not Egyptian, given this background, I'm asserting my claims and seeking reparations for historical injustices.

The earth is flooding worldwide. The earth is crying tears water all over; this is sad because water represents people multitude nations and countries 😥 everywhere you see water represents the tears of real people the ancestors are disturb for everything that have happened to them 💔 earth reflects our inner selves; our bodies reflect the earth's mother nature and our minds thoughts mindset represents the universe.... See Isaiah 42:13-16.

The earth is experiencing widespread flooding, and it's as if the planet is crying tears of water everywhere. This is a poignant reminder that water often symbolizes the multitude of people, nations, and countries. Wherever we see water, it can represent the tears and struggles of real people. The ancestors seem to be disturbed by the injustices and harm they've endured.

The earth can be seen as a reflection of our inner selves – our physical bodies mirroring the natural world and our minds and thoughts reflecting the universe. This interconnectedness is profound. As it says in Isaiah 42:13-16, the Lord will march forth like a mighty man, stir up his zeal like a warrior, and will shout, yes, raise a war cry; he will prevail against his enemies.

Narcissistic individuals often focus intently on their goals and cultivate strategic connections. I don't see anything inherently wrong with having a strong sense of self-importance or ambition, and I don't believe in feigning humility. Instead, I prioritize fairness and equality in all aspects of life. For me, it's about recognizing one's worth and advocating for oneself while still treating others with respect and dignity.

After slavery was abolished on paper, many freed slaves found themselves without the means to support themselves. As a result, some signed contracts to become indentured servants, working without wages in exchange for basic necessities like food, water, clothing, and shelter. This arrangement often meant that they were still trapped in a cycle of labor with little to no opportunity for progress or advancement.

In many ways, the outcome of slavery, indentured servitude, and modern-day employment can feel similar – working just enough to cover basic needs without truly gaining ground in life. This realization is part of why I've chosen to forge my own path. I'm driven by choice, and I've chosen to dedicate myself to writing spiritual awakening books. For me, autonomy and purpose are more valuable than any traditional job.

I can imagine how so many people continue during the ages to try to make a difference and their efforts were down size to nothing as they were buried and forgotten in society because the very people who they were trying to reach with the knowledge of spiritual ascension, did not believe in the caused they saw no need to learn about spirituality and self-discovery. People are more concerned about what they'll wear next and eat next; people love living in the darkness of this underworld;

people seek out to take booster shots in the face of all the negativity side effects that will happen to you if you take it. It's like taking AZT medication for aids recovery when AZT was offered you to finish you off.

People are Sims, just existing in the system, simple here today and gone tomorrow.

Will my work books fall on deaf ears and be forgotten 😕 why cast pearls to undeserving swine human pigs who careless about truths spirituality ascension nor care about anything of spirituality? The earth got to purge of its infidels.

I often wonder how many people throughout history have tried to make a difference, only to have their efforts diminished and forgotten. Those who sought to share knowledge of spiritual ascension were often met with skepticism and disinterest by the very people they were trying to help. It seems that many are more concerned with material pursuits, such as what to wear or eat next, rather than seeking spiritual growth and self-discovery. Some people appear to be comfortable living in the darkness of this world, and they'll even take risks with their health by opting for treatments with potential negative side effects.

It's disheartening to see people existing in the system without purpose, like pawns in a game. They're here today and gone tomorrow, without any deeper understanding or connection to spirituality. I worry that my work, including my books, might fall on deaf ears and be forgotten. Why share valuable insights with those who don't appreciate or care about spiritual truths and ascension?

Perhaps the earth needs to undergo a transformation, purging itself of those who refuse to awaken to its true nature.

As an author of spiritual manifestations, one of the first questions people tend to ask me is: How do I manifest money and prosperity??? My answer is I never ever asked you for money. We need to breathe to live. We need health, water, food, and a shelter from the elements. Money paper dollars will soon be laying worthless in the streets, and nobody will be picking them up. Earth is the only planet where the bottom line for everything is money, money to love and to be in a relationship, money to breathe, money to be buried. In the coming new earth there won't be money exchanges; we will practice sustainable farming and maintaining project development for free water engineering and technology to harness free electricity; no taxes, no lies, no white washing, no deceptions. There will be a day of reckoning for this present global system and we will go back to the way of living from ancient taratirans civilizations where everything was free so we can collectively concentrate on knowledge truths as we be enjoying life.

As an author of spiritual manifestos, one of the first questions people tend to ask me is: "How do I manifest money and prosperity?" My response is that I've never asked money for anything meaningful. We need to breathe to live. We need health, water, food, and shelter from the elements. Paper dollars will soon be rendered worthless, and no one will bother picking them up soon. Money will be scattered worthless on the streets. Earth is unique in that everything seems to revolve around money – money for love, relationships, breathing (in the sense of healthcare), and even burial.

However, in the emerging new Earth, we won't be trading in monetary exchanges. Instead, we'll adopt sustainable farming practices and collaborative project development, harnessing free water engineering and technology to generate electricity without cost. There will be no taxes, no deceit, no manipulation, and no false pretenses. A reckoning is coming for the current global systems, and we'll return to a way of living reminiscent of ancient civilizations where resources were shared freely. This shift will allow us to focus on enjoying and experiencing life together.

See if you have just one drop of black bloodline genes in you; then you are identified as black. We really cannot judge people by the color of their skin hair eyes, we are now a hybrid mixture of the races, and we cannot really determine anyone's origin based on outward appearances. I, author Lindbergh Sedacy, welcome you all to my posts messages writings books and groups without prejudice.

Consider this: if you have just one drop of black ancestry in your genetic makeup, you're often identified as black. This highlights the arbitrary nature of judging people based on skin color, hair texture, or eye color. Given the increasing hybridization of races, outward appearances can be misleading, and it's challenging to determine someone's origin solely by looking at them. As the author, Lindbergh Sedacy, I extend a warm welcome to all who engage with my posts, messages, writings, books, and groups – free from prejudice and judgment.

Elohim are independent individuals who will stop at nothing to reach to the peoples with the ultimate truths of Yahweh's guidance and salvation. They will sacrifice themselves to deliver the messages of truths to the general public... John 3:16.

The Elohim are unwavering messengers who tirelessly share the ultimate truths of Yahweh's guidance and salvation with humanity. With unrelenting dedication, they sacrifice themselves to deliver these life-changing messages to the public, as reflected in John 3:16: 'For God so loved the world that he gave his begotten Sons and daughters, that whoever believes in Yahweh shall not perish but have eternal life.

If the devil would make a confession about the spiritual writer who has come closer towards the universal truths in his writings and books; he would say author Mr. Lindbergh Sedacy narrative is next to the ultimate truths closer than anyone else, yes closer than ever.

If the devil were to make a confession about the spiritual writer who has come closest to the universal truths in their writings and books, he would say that author Mr. Lindbergh Sedacy's narrative is remarkably close to the ultimate truths – closer than anyone else, even closest than anyone else has ever been. Author Lindbergh Sedacy is a decoder of the codes the knowledge of the codes is the key to uncovering the universal laws author Lindbergh Sedacy Spiritual books is, he is the solution...Genesis 41:45; Isaiah 52:13-15;44:5,7.

As a younger man I was big and buff, after years have passed I age and my body got smaller. One day I was walking then suddenly I felt my 27-year-old body had returned to me and I felt my strength my confidence I knew I had powers and I felt as a god......what caused this remembrance that took on my former physical attributes why can't I summon this strength to come to me when I need it? So many things I need to learn that will help me on my journey and pathway in life that can truly let me live and function as the Elohim God that: I AM.

As a younger man, I was physically strong and fit, but as the years went by, I aged and my body changed. However, I had a profound experience where I suddenly felt my 27-year-old body return to me. I regained a sense of strength, confidence, and power, feeling almost divine.

The question remains: what triggered this temporary rejuvenation, and why can't I tap into that strength whenever I need it? There's still much for me to learn and discover on my life's journey, and I'm eager to uncover the secrets that will help me grow and thrive.

A 'snake' can be someone you consider a friend, yet they exhibit deceptive and cold behavior towards you. True purpose in life goes beyond serving religion or being religious; it's about spirituality – recognizing your connection to every living being. To live with purpose, be kind to both animals and people, and remember that charity begins at home. Wish peace for others and cultivate inner peace as you work towards your contributions to the world and not focus only on enjoying life.

When you're aligned with your purpose, you'll feel an unexplainable passion that compels you to act. Purpose is your mission, the reason you're here on earth. It's not just about chasing money, fame, or fortune; it's often about helping others and guiding them on their own path to self-discovery and spiritual growth.

If you don't follow your purpose, you might miss out on a fulfilling life. The universe appreciates your contributions, regardless of whether others recognize them. So, keep believing in yourself and your worth. Your purpose will reveal itself through your passions and inner guidance – trust in that process.

When I revisited the Bible, I can now see that Yahushua was a spiritualist he practiced spirituality with a background of Judaism; Is exactly who I am today. Christianity is no longer offered at my table; it's only primitive minds still following Christianity that was forced upon our ancestors and passed down to us from the colonizers. So many People refuse to be awakened from sleeping the light has come it is here. Genesis 1:3.

Upon revisiting the Bible, I've come to see Yahushua as a spiritualist who practiced spirituality within the context of Judaism. This resonates with my own spiritual path today. I've moved beyond traditional Christianity, recognizing it as a legacy of our colonized past that was imposed upon our ancestors.

Many people remain unaware of the deeper truths, still caught in the cycle of sleep. But the light of awareness is here, offering a chance for awakening. As Genesis 1:3 reminds us, 'Let there be light,' and so it is.

Just remember that the future goal for sati light fifteen minutes zone cities is for no private personal transportations.

So, the ownership of vicheles will at some point will be discouraged and the system will be stopped us in our tracks from driving; welcome a new era to the avaliablity of public transportations; nowhere to run nowhere to hide, no private vicheles to get out. The price to import vicheles to third world countries taxes of import duty will be so high causing average people not to own private vicheles. In these final years ahead, the concept of communities will be forever changing and every country in the world internationally will be forced to follow suit.

Looking ahead, the future vision for smart cities includes a shift towards reduced private transportation. In these '15-minute cities,' the goal is to encourage reliance on public transportation, potentially discouraging personal vehicle ownership. This could mark a new era in urban mobility, where walking, cycling, and public transport became the norm. The idea is to create more efficient, sustainable, and community-focused living spaces.

When you're facing bills are pressing upon you; do not sell your soul, do not compromise your values; down size if you must, but don't you ever quit. What's important to you is to keep on breathing, not image, not pride of life, not bills not having a car; you value is life to keep on breathing for God only dwells inside of the living, not in the dead.

When survival bills weigh heavily on you, don't compromise your values or sell your soul. If necessary, downsize, but never give up. What's truly important is preserving life, not maintaining an image, pride, or paying bills. Your value lies in staying alive, for the divine presence dwells within the living, not the dead.

Money, greed, pride, lust, theft, betrayals base on success or having a successful image; are the down fall of mankind and is the reason that the earth is referred to be the underworld where human vampires feeds off its inhabitants.

Money, greed, pride, lust, theft, and betrayal – often driven by the pursuit of success or a successful image – can be the downfall of humanity. These negative traits may contribute to the Earth being seen as an 'underworld' where destructive forces feed off its inhabitants, causing harm pain suffering sorrows frustration anger betrayal disappointments is hell on earth; amidst all of the chaos the kingdom of heaven is within us; uni-one unity united front creating peaceful settlements is a starting point.

Try to understand yourself.... you have an energy you have frequency you have vibration; constantly emitting from your presence to the universe ✨ when you come across people who doesn't really know you but they refuse to be a friend this is because your frequencies don't match. When it seems like you can't find a partner in life it's because you are one of a kind in this realm and no one comes close compatibility of your elohim presence. Just let them be; you will eventually find your twin flame your soul mate sooner or later if not in this underworld then in another realm in another probability where you also exist you found love. Never force anything to happen just be your authentic self-recognizing that you are Elohim a god in the flesh and most people will not adjust nor relate to you ✨.

Understanding yourself is key. You possess a unique energy, frequency, and vibration that constantly emit from your presence to the universe. When you encounter people, who don't know you but refuse to connect, it might be due to mismatched frequencies. If finding a life partner seems challenging, it's possible that you're one of a kind in this realm, and your Elohim presence is unmatched.

Instead of forcing on connections, focus on being your authentic self, recognizing your divine nature. Your twin flame or soulmate might be waiting in this realm or another, in a different probability where you exist. Trust that you'll find love when the time is right. Until then, embrace your uniqueness and let others be – your path will unfold naturally.

Our thoughts aren't truly ours; they just pop into our minds. This implies that our thoughts aren't original, which raises a profound question: if our thoughts are influenced by external factors without our conscious awareness, does that mean we're being controlled subconsciously? This idea resonates with the philosophical notion that the concept of a unified self is an illusion, echoing the phrase 'there ain't no me' - suggesting that our sense of individual identity might be more flaws than we think.

What say you about this Post?

The answer is: We are all collectively connected and being control either for good or for evil by the exclusive embodiment of the Elohim Gods who are us; Yah residence inside ourselves and in unity and togetherness we manifest One God, One = Yahweh.

Under ground is our only protection from what are coming ahead; is a nuclear nightmare a radiation nightmare not returning to the surface of the earth for over a thousand years. Will the wealthy people survive 😳 Got to give them A for efforts 🖐 but they'll not survive a thousand years the only selection of peoples who will emerge alive after a thousand years are the ones selection on the harvest of the rapture and were placed in underground spaceships to bunkers down until the calamities on the surface of earth be over passed and after a thousand years out of the ashes we will rise and rebuild a new governance where the Elohim Gods makes and set the laws and not potentially corrupt human beings. This is the coming reset will begin either November 9th, in the year 2097-or in the year-2112 but by the year 2113 the earth is depopulated of human beings; leaving only robots reptilians and alien visitors. The surface of the earth will be contaminated with atomic radiation for a century; only in Eden can one survive for a thousand years said author Mr. Lindbergh Sedacy he encourages you to read his books entitled: My Skin Hurts by Lindbergh Sedacy purchase on online platforms around the world.

The underground is our only protection from what's coming ahead – a nuclear and radiation nightmare that will render the Earth's surface uninhabitable for over a thousand years. It's uncertain whether wealthy individuals will survive. While they may make efforts to prepare, it's unlikely they'll endure for a thousand years.

Only a select group, often referred to as the "harvest" or "rapture," will emerge alive after this period. These individuals will be sheltered in underground bunkers in healing center called Myra that are spaceships design to keep the Elohim Israelites brothers and sisters alive until the calamities on the surface pass. After a thousand years, they will rise and rebuild a new governance, with the Elohim governance will be setting and making the laws of the new reset the new world.

According to author Lindbergh Sedacy interpretations, this reset may occur between November 9th, 2097, and 2112, with the Earth being definitely depopulated by 2113, leaving behind robots, reptilians, animals and alien visitors. The surface will be contaminated with atomic radiation for centuries. As stated, "Only in Eden can one survive for a thousand years. Read my book entitled: The Children of Eden in the Hills of Belize it will explain more about the gardens of Eden.

By the way, thank you for reading my latest book, "The Elohims, Gods they are walking in the flesh amongst us by Lindbergh Sedacy"

Yahoo Mail: Search, Organize, Conquer

My cash App account info is: $Belize2008.

PayPal and Zella account: Sedacylindbergh77@yahoo.com

Merchant account: Elavon Lindbergh Sedacy Sr

Mailbox & Mailing address: 809 wests 23rd street #17 Los Angeles CA 90007.

Payment method for purchasing author Lindbergh Sedacy Spiritual books.

Kindly email me your personal address leaving Payment information and which book you're ordering for. Cost price for any of my books 📚 is us$24.95

Thanks, you for reading: The Elohim Gods.

Many are so connected to religion living a religious life serving the churches that caused them to fail to hear the voices of the ancestors crying out for justice. These ancestors were silenced and killed their blood spilled by colonizers who imposed their religious beliefs through force. When we don't lend our support in the cause of change our ancestors who are still waiting in graves all over the earth asking for justice: How much longer must we wait for justice to come to us, the earth will keep crying tears, manifesting in floods and other natural disasters.

To our ancestors who lie in their graves, awaiting the justice they deserve, you will have to wait a little longer. According to the prophecy, the end will come on November 9th, 2097, or 2112. By 2113, the earth shall be depopulated of wicked people and those who suffered in the graves shall be completely avenged all those who suffered exploitation based on slavery, displacement, and the stramer of losing children and love ones been rape molested and their true identity stolen by white imposters Revelation 2:9;3:9.

The awakened Elohim individuals are here and a flood of youths called the princes and princesses of the new spiritual covenant shall come like a flood and will override Babylon with truths, away with her confusion deceptions and stronghold on the peoples, the lies of Babylon all will be revealed, the old ways and the ancient wisdom of our ancestors shall return like stars resemble plasma intelligent balls of lights, alive and round in shape, has the appearance of the reflection of light through water called orbs in the sky. At the end of the day, each person will make their own choice, and regardless of decisions, it won't stop the changes that are coming. those who remain neutral will be asked to choose a side, can you join the movement of the Elohims, and counteract those who spread negativity and religious lies and bigotry.

The human brain, as a collective consciousness, functions as a dynamic database of the universe, integrating and processing vast amounts of information that mirror the complexities of existence of people. This interconnected network of multitude of people's prayer requests embodies the cumulative in the database, of the experiences, and sorrows of humanity are recorded, effectively serving as a repository which is a database of universal cries hurts and pain of humanity ascended prayers are been processed as the universe listen and records everyone prayers request their anger betrayal disappointments frustrations loss hurts pain sorrows as it's resonate throughout the heavens and the earth, prayers are gathered in the universe database. Everything is interconnected and alive – from rocks and bricks to sand, stones, and wood – all capable of reconfiguring themselves in response to the universe's demands that is a reflection and the manifestation of the Elohim brothers and sisters, who are the embodiment of the Gods alive within the flesh as they walk on the surface of the world. ELOHIM means GODS, but in unity as a united front all breathing. " Ye-Ha = let every life let every breathe be in togetherness be silent and know that you are Elohim gods".

As a collective Elohims consciousness in unity, this privatized the fulfillment of the return of Christ who had to go away so can return and now can be everywhere in everyplace at the same time all over the face of the earth, and together as in one aim one goal one understanding one united front one movement one belief one baptism they're One God "Yahweh" so the engathering of Israel will come (Isaiah 11: 10-12) when this happens it will be game over for the evil monsters and rulers even for the reptilians who feed off the negativity of human beings suffering in this underworld.

I'm unwavering in my stance, and no amount of wealth could change my position. Some things are priceless. The momentum for change is unstoppable, like a wildfire that consumes everything in its path. Many who love the business of church are afraid of seeing their churches institutions and organizations be destroyed by my messages of spirituality and many good people like brother Smith of the SDA church in Los Angeles CA next to the freeway they (he) don't realize that the return of Christ symbolizes a spiritual awakening transformation and ascension of a small crowd of people that thinks outside of the box religion, just a few awakened Christ consciousness explaining spirituality will transform the world by challenging the deceptions of religious institutions.

The white hispanards didn't see anything special about the Mayans' writings and destroyed them; the same attitude with spirituality today they are the least concerned. Spirituality are the sciences of the ancient people's ancient civilizations that was lost and now this knowledge is making its way back to modern day advance mankind where black people are relatively connecting with these sacred truths also known to be laws.

The conquistadors showed little appreciation for the significance of Mayan writings and destroyed many of them. Similarly, today, some people remain largely uninterested in spirituality. Spirituality represents the ancient sciences and knowledge of bygone civilizations that were lost over time. However, this knowledge is now resurfacing, and many people, including those of black African and black native indigenous Indian descent, are reconnecting with these sacred truths and laws.

Lindbergh Sedacy has a blend of the biblical account and spirituality. Personally author Lindbergh Sedacy believe that the church has failed us/him; so many are attending church living a double life so many are literal devils and should not be attending church and should be excommunicated the church should be a house for prayers but has become a den of Satanism where the righteous saints are exploited and bitten destroyed by fake members who careless about truths salvation nor people and many sincere upright members are bitten by the snakes of the church that their ending is worse than when they first joined the church searching salvation, it was better that they never enter salvation by church and after the negative experience by church they lifted, many will turn to spirituality that is to flee the churches enter your own private closets and pray in your secret private chamber so many in solitude find God within themselves and was rewarded openly as they walk as gods, for many will do self-discovery selfcare got to understand that they've already immortal souls and death has no claim upon them; for the Elohim brothers and sisters death is life; only our bodies dies our souls are eternal we can transform our souls into new hosts new bodies we can return back to earth when we chooses to; the churches cannot offer us salvation we are Elohim gods with immortal souls.

Let me share a little history about myself concerning my journey so far: My name is Lindbergh Sedacy Sr. My ancestral roots trace back to Ethiopia, specifically the province of Gondar, where my people originated as black Falasha Jews. Over time, they migrated to the east of Ethiopia, which was renamed India and later renamed Pakistan, and my grandparents traveled by ship in central America before eventually settings in Belize formerly British Honduras, where I was born on August 1st, 1965 at an seventh day Adventist hospital; my mother had complications in giving birth her baby and Macquarie SDA hospital helped me into this world.

On July 1st, 2008, I relocated to the United States and found residence in South Central Los Angeles, California. It was here that I met my wife and began writing spiritual awakening books. My wife supported me against great odds she met me was genuinely drawn to me and found out I did not have documents to be in America she found out that I was sleeping in my car and took me home with her to her 1.9 million dollar house and supported me financially as I Initially wrote, my first book it was a Bible study self-help guides, entitled: 'My Skin Hurts,' a biblical exploration of black history.

I am grateful to my ex-wife, Miss Dorothy Saldono, we were married on (October 21st,2011) She initially helped me out when I first arrived in Los Angeles, CA.

She still after our divorce (September 06th, 2024) check up on me; her family never truly accepted me, so I walked away in 2019 seeking a future with a church gal named Eve who sold me a happily ever after dream but ghosted me and walked away leaving me abandoned as if I was trashed and she didn't consider my happiness I was discarded. I walked away from my established wife, and then I was ghosted by a church attending pretender who enjoyed a double life. Yes, I was played like a fidel she played me like a chess game of shame she became the rottenness in my bones, leaving me bewildered and lost in the sauce of disappointment frustrations, anger, pain betrayals brokenness and nobody cared, it took me years to recover from my devastation five years exactly.

My marriage with Dorothy was not perfect, but she was better than most that I have encountered; after Eve, I remained and lived single. My ex-wife had powdered me and spoiled me, and this changed my prospective views on dating women. I should have kept my wife. Good people out here are hard to find essential, especially at my age.....

At some points, Sedacy emerged both Bible and spirituality in his spiritually awakening books.

When you're doing a great job and feeling confident, haters often emerge, trying to derail my progress. However, my purpose, destiny, and life were predestined long before my birth, as written in the book of Isaiah 4:2:11:1-3;29:10-15,18-24;41:2,27;52:7. I've been called, chosen, selected, and prepared for this task. Yes, I am silent as a lamb. I am a fearless lion, but I lay down once low like a helpless lamb when in church attendance. won't create any divisions, not on my watch. I realize I am not compatible with most so I wait for the opportunity to purchase my own building and start a spiritual center to serves the Los Angeles community; yes, I am quite and I will step up when the time arise to emerge as a great leader that will be respected internationally see Isaiah 32:1. No obstacle, not even the gates of hell, can stop spirituality. We'll navigate through challenges, over, under, around, or straight through them.

As I stand at the pinnacle of spiritual genius, it's lonely on the top, I'm inviting you to join me on this journey. All it takes is commitment dedication as in a marriage relationship Isaiah 4:1. Remember, the universe reflects our inner selves. Know yourself, and understand that our mindset can change outwards probabilities together we can change situations and the external world. Let be the change we want to see, starting from within.

If you're interested in exploring spirituality and personal growth, I'd like to invite you to check out my books, including:

"The Awakened Ones"

"My Skin Hurts"

"The Children of Eden in the Hills of Belize"

"Are You A Star Seed?"

"Chosen One"

"Elohim"

These titles are available on Google, Amazon, Barnes & Noble, and other online platforms worldwide. Written by Lindbergh Sedacy Sr., they offer insights into the distinctions and connections between religion and spirituality.

AUTHOR LINDBERGH SEDACY

Kindly take a picture

of my book and QR

code.May this connection

solidify your personal Support is

appreciated

Thank You!!

Lindbergh Sedacy

Send Money with Zelle®

Scan in your banking app to pay

Scan to pay with Cash App

Lindbergh Samuel Sedacy Jr

s***7@yahoo.com

PayPal

LindberghSedacySr
$Belize2008

Scan. Pay. Go.

Zelle

Visa and Mastercard Accepted